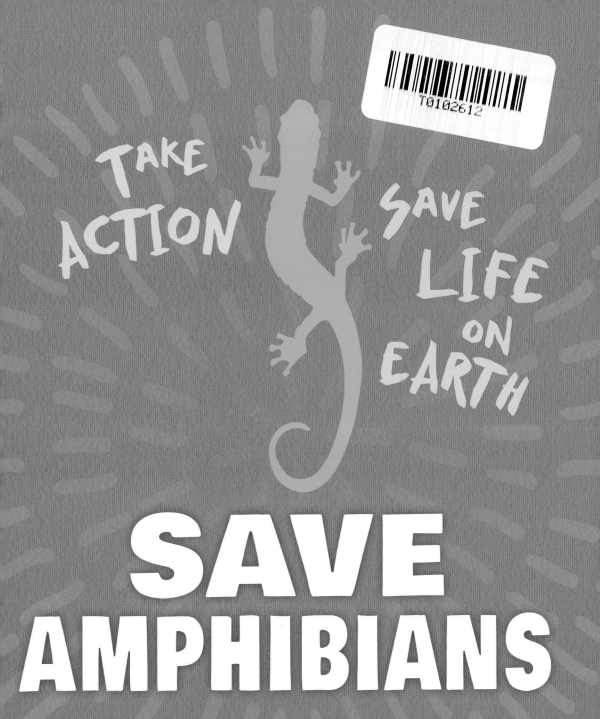

TAKE
ACTION

SAVE
LIFE
ON
EARTH

SAVE
AMPHIBIANS

Stephanie Feldstein

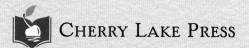

Published in the United States of America by Cherry Lake Publishing Group
Ann Arbor, Michigan
www.cherrylakepublishing.com

Reading Adviser: Beth Walker Gambro, MS, Ed., Reading Consultant, Yorkville, IL
Book Designer: Felicia Macheske

Photo Credits: © Steve Bower/Shutterstock, cover; © IrinaK/Shutterstock, 4; © kamolwan Aimpongpaitoon/ Shutterstock, 13; © Matt Ragen/Shutterstock, © Erickson Stock/Shutterstock, 17; © Mike Wilhelm/Shutterstock, 18; © Brian Gratwicke via Flickr, Attribution 2.0 Generic (CC BY 2.0) Ecnomiohyla rabborum (Rabb's Fringe-limbed Treefrog), 20; © Matt Richards, 21; © Freebird7977/Shutterstock, 23; © Michael Sundberg/Shutterstock, 25; © Alex Popov/Shutterstock, 26; © NITINAI THABTHONG/Shutterstock, 29; © Wirestock Creators/Shutterstock, back cover; © xpixel/Shutterstock, back cover

Graphics Credits: © AVIcon/Shutterstock; © VladimirCeresnak/Shutterstock; © Pavel K/Shutterstock; Panimoni/ Shutterstock; © Hulinska Yevheniia/Shutterstock; © Vector Place/Shutterstock; © davooda/Shutterstock

Cherry Lake Press is an imprint of Cherry Lake Publishing Group.

Library of Congress Cataloging-in-Publication Data has been filed and is available at catalog.loc.gov.

Cherry Lake Publishing Group would like to acknowledge the work of the Partnership for 21st Century Learning, a Network of Battelle for Kids. Please visit *http://www.battelleforkids.org/networks/p21* for more information.

Printed in the United States of America
Corporate Graphics

Note from publisher: Websites change regularly, and their future contents are outside of our control. Supervise children when conducting any recommended online searches for extended learning opportunities.

Table of Contents

INTRODUCTION
Amphibians and the Extinction Crisis

Hellbenders seem like creatures from a story. They live at the bottom of rivers and streams. They're flat and slimy. They're as big as 2 feet (0.6 meters) long. They have funny nicknames like snot otters. They breathe through their skin.

But hellbenders are real animals. They're a type of salamander. Salamanders are **amphibians**. Amphibians live in and near fresh water. They're cold-blooded animals. That means their body temperature changes with their surroundings. Most amphibians spend part of their lives in water and part on land. Frogs, toads, and salamanders are all amphibians.

More than 41 percent of the world's amphibians are at risk of **extinction**. This is when all of one kind of plant or animal dies. It affects wild plants and animals. An extinct plant or animal is gone forever. Scientists say we're in an extinction **crisis**. We miss out when wildlife goes extinct.

It weakens **ecosystems**. Healthy ecosystems make food, shelter, water, and clean air. Life on Earth needs all kinds of plants and animals.

Amphibians need fresh water. Most amphibians lay their eggs in water. Their **larvae** grow up there. Some amphibians **hibernate** under water. This is to survive the cold weather.

Amphibians don't actually drink water. They absorb it through their skin. It helps them get the oxygen they need. They can't breathe if their skin gets too dry. Their skin is very sensitive. They can't survive without clean water. Water pollution can poison them.

We can stop the extinction crisis. People need to take action. Governments need to act, too. By working together, we can save amphibians.

Why We Need
AMPHIBIANS

Amphibians aren't the only ones who need fresh water. Plants and animals need it to live. That includes humans. Some amphibians are **indicator species**. Indicator species are very sensitive to their environment. They're like a warning system. The **ecosystem** is in trouble if they're not healthy. If amphibians don't have fresh water, neither do we.

Amphibians are an important part of the food chain. Their larvae feed on vegetation. Adults eat insects. They keep plants and bugs in balance. Amphibians are eaten by larger animals like birds. Fish, snakes, lizards, and other animals eat them, too.

Saving amphibians saves freshwater ecosystems. Humans and other animals need amphibians to survive.

CHAPTER ONE

Amphibians on the Brink

Disappearing **habitat** is the biggest threat to amphibians. Habitat is the place where wild animals live. Amphibian habitat is destroyed to build new places. Wetlands are drained to form dry land. Then houses and other buildings are built on top. Amphibians can't live there anymore.

Amphibians are sensitive. They can live only in fresh water. They get sick when water is polluted. Freshwater ecosystems are polluted by **runoff**. Runoff is when the ground can't absorb rain. It flows into nearby waterways. It carries chemicals and dirt. Runoff from buildings and roads is harmful. It makes the water cloudy. This is called **sedimentation**. Freshwater plants and animals can't survive in cloudy water.

Amphibians, like this leopard frog, need fresh water. They spend part of their life in water and part on land.

TURNING POINT

Dissection is cutting open a dead animal to study it. Millions of frogs are dissected in science classes every year. Some may be taken from the wild. This practice may harm both frogs and freshwater ecosystems.

In 1987, Jenifer Graham was a 15-year-old student in California. She didn't want to dissect a frog. She thought it was cruel. Her teacher wouldn't give her a different assignment. Jenifer took the school to court. Her case made California change its law. Students could refuse to dissect animals. Teachers had to give them different assignments. Now more than 20 states have laws that let students choose not to dissect.

Students can use models and computer programs instead. They learn about the frog's body without dissecting one. These alternatives can save millions of frogs each year.

Frogs have often been used to teach anatomy. There are now ways to teach anatomy without killing animals.

Runoff from farms also carries **pesticides**. Pesticides are **toxic** chemicals made to kill things like weeds or bugs that farmers don't want on fields. But they also kill wildlife. They poison amphibians through their skin.

More than half of U.S. rivers and streams are polluted. It's not healthy for people to drink. It's dangerous to swim or fish there. It's bad for amphibians and other animals, too.

Dissection alternatives are better for the environment. They can be used more than once. They don't take wild animals from their homes. They're also safer for students. Animals used for dissection are treated with chemicals. These chemicals can harm people.

Some schools use computer programs that simulate frog dissection. Others have detailed models. These are made from clay or plastic. In 2019, a Florida high school was the first to use synthetic frogs. They look just like frogs. Students use them to learn without harming any frogs.

Climate change also harms amphibians. Warmer temperatures dry up water. Stronger storms cause more runoff. That creates more sedimentation.

Millions of frogs and other amphibians are taken from the wild every year. They're kept as pets. They're used in classrooms and science labs. This disrupts whole ecosystems. It pushes amphibians closer to extinction.

◀ Warmer temperatures and drought caused by climate change have dried up this lake in Oregon.

CHAPTER TWO

Save Water for Wildlife

Climate change is drying up fresh water. Warm, dry weather leads to **drought**. That's when there's not enough rain for a long period of time. There's not enough water for plants, animals, and people.

Expanding towns and farms make the problem worse. More people need more water. More farm animals and crops need more water. Everyone is trying to share the same resources. It's drying up amphibian habitat.

We need water to drink, bathe, cook, and clean. But we often don't think about where it comes from. The average American family uses more than 300 gallons (1,136 liters) of water each day. Being thoughtful about how we use it can help save water for wildlife.

Running faucets can waste more than 2 gallons (8 L) of water every minute. Turning it off when brushing your teeth can save almost 3–4 gallons (11–15 L) per person per day. Taking shorter showers helps, too. Making your shower just two minutes shorter can save 5 gallons (19 L) of water. Dishwashers use less water than hand-washing dishes. If you have a dishwasher, load it up.

You can help save water by turning off water while brushing your teeth.

Frogger was one of the first video games with an animal that needed to cross a busy road. Frogger had to dodge traffic to reach a safe home on the other side.

Some amphibians need to cross roads in real life. They live most of the year on one side of the road. But the water where they lay eggs is on the other side. They're not fast enough to dodge cars.

Scientists and volunteers help the amphibians. The helpers wait until the weather is right. It's usually a cool, rainy spring night. They try to catch the amphibians before they get to the road. They carry as many as they can to safety.

It's also important to stop leaks. One leaky faucet can waste 3,000 gallons (11,356 L) of water every year. Tell your parents if you notice a leak so they can fix it.

Farming is the biggest water user. Meat and dairy farms need a lot of water. It's used for the animals and the crops they eat. Plants don't need as much water to grow. It takes more than 880 gallons (3,331 L) of water to make one glass of dairy milk. A hamburger uses 15 times more water than a veggie burger. Eating less meat and dairy helps save water.

Using less water leaves more for amphibians. But you can also protect their habitat from pollution. Products like cleaners and paints have toxic chemicals in them. They're called **hazardous** waste. Don't pour them down the drain. The chemicals could wind up back in rivers and streams. There are places to get rid of hazardous waste. Find out how to dispose of it in your community.

CONSERVATION CHAMPIONS

A fungus was killing frogs in Panama. The frogs were an **endangered species**. They were in danger of extinction. Dozens were rescued from the forest. They were sent to places where they could get special care.

Rabbs' fringe-limbed tree frogs were brown frogs. They had big, webbed feet. There weren't any left in the wild. Most of them died from the fungus. Mark Mandica worked for the Atlanta Botanical Garden. He cared for the last Rabbs' fringe-limbed tree frog in the world.

Mandica's son, Anthony, named the last Rabb's fringe-limbed tree frog "Toughie." The Mandicas knew Toughie wouldn't live forever. When Toughie died in 2016, his species went extinct.

But Mandica and his son didn't give up on saving amphibians. Mark, Anthony, and Crystal Mandica started the Amphibian Foundation. They educate people about the amphibians they love. They teach people of all ages how to help them. They do research with other **conservation** experts. Conservation is action to protect wildlife and nature. The Mandica family is learning how we can better protect amphibians.

The family also cares for other endangered species. They work to save their habitat. They're making the world safer for these special animals.

Amphibians face an extinction crisis. The Mandica family brings hope for their future.

Mark Mandica on a sampling expedition to study endangered salamanders in Georgia

CHAPTER THREE

Citizen Science

Amphibians are some of the most threatened animals on Earth. They're disappearing faster than scientists can study them.

Experts need more information about amphibians in the wild. They need to know how many there are. They need to know where they live. They need to track the health of wetlands and streams.

Experts are training people to gather information on amphibians. This is called citizen science. Volunteers learn about amphibians in their area. They learn about local wetlands. Communities work with scientists to save them.

Scientists test water to check the health of lakes, rivers, and ponds.

SPEAK UP FOR AMPHIBIANS

Millions of people keep amphibians as pets. Some are bred ethically in an effort to help conserve a species in the wild. However, many of them are taken from the wild. Then they're sold to pet stores. The pet trade that involves taking amphibians from the wild is a huge threat to amphibians. The people collecting them spread deadly diseases. Amphibian populations can't recover. The ecosystems that need them suffer.

Here's how you can help stop this unethical pet trade:

1. Encourage your friends not to get unethically-bred (wild-caught) pet amphibians. Nature needs amphibians in the wild. Some pet stores say their animals were bred in captivity. You can ask them if their amphibians were bred ethically. Many breeders start with wild amphibians.

Wild amphibians should be left alone. They are not pets.

2 Ask pet stores to stop selling unethically-bred amphibians. Wild animals don't belong in stores. Look up the company's email address online. Write a letter to the company's leaders. Tell them why amphibians are important. Explain how the unethical pet trade harms amphibians. Ask your friends to write letters, too. You can mail your letters. You can email them. You can deliver them to the store manager.

Wild amphibians aren't pets. They need you to help spread the word.

Pet amphibians are usually collected from faraway places. They don't belong in your local pond or stream. They could hurt native wildlife. They could change the whole ecosystem. And they might not know how to survive there.

Never release a pet amphibian into the wild if you're unable to keep it. Some local animal shelters will take in pet amphibians. There may also be amphibian rescue groups near you. They'll make sure they're safe and don't harm the ecosystem.

One program is called FrogWatch USA. It's run by zoos and aquariums. More than 15,000 people participate in FrogWatch. They learn to listen for frogs and toads. They identify different species by their ribbits and croaks. They collect data on what they hear. Researchers study the data. It helps them understand how many kinds of amphibians are in an area. It helps them figure out how best to save them.

Another program is the Global Amphibian BioBlitz. Citizen scientists use a nature app called iNaturalist. People look for wildlife in their area. They take photos of what they see. The app helps them identify plants and animals. Scientists use these observations to help save wildlife. People have logged more than 1.7 million observations just about amphibians.

Some communities create nature challenges. They get groups of people to participate. They gather a lot of data all at once. Some teachers use citizen science in their classrooms. Students learn how to observe wildlife. Sometimes classes learn to test water where amphibians live. They test for chemicals that might be harmful.

Citizen scientists help protect whole ecosystems.

A field trip for a science class can help scientists ▶ learn how amphibians are doing where you live.

CREATE A BACKYARD AMPHIBIAN SANCTUARY

Frogs, toads, and salamanders often stop by gardens. They're excellent guests. They eat bugs that could harm your plants. They might even sing to you. But they need you to make it safe for them.

1 Don't use pesticides to kill bugs or weeds. The chemicals can harm amphibian visitors. It can also seep into their habitat.